Selling the Mark of the Beast

Marketing RFID: EU vs. US

June Dawn Knight

This book exposes the enemy's plan to implant a microchip into each human. This RFID tag is the Mark of the Beast in the Book of Revelation.

Copyright © 2015 June Dawn Knight
Published by

All rights reserved.
ISBN: 1505704421
ISBN-13: 978-1505704426

DEDICATION

This book is dedicated to my mother, Wilma (JJ) Bracey and my grandmother, Cora Ann Milam Jenner. Thank you for your prayers and support in my journey with the Lord Jesus Christ. My grandmother passed away in the 70s and I can still feel her prayers today. My mother is my rock and I am so thankful for the love and standing by my side in the good and bad. Love you mom!

BOOK REVIEWS

There are watchmen on the wall sounding the alarm in many different areas of life. Whether they are sounding the alarm in the natural or in the spiritual, each one is given different gifts from God that are used even when we don't realize it. If you are interested in something, it probably has something to do with one of your gifts from God.

June Dawn Knight had a desire to write about the subject of the mark of the beast before she ever dreamed it would be in book form. But isn't that how God works? When He gives us something, He always wants the world to know what He is saying, for He lives in us through His Holy Spirit and is our guide. Jesus said it is better for you that I go away so that the Holy Spirit can live inside of you.

There is a place in God's word that says He orders our steps and I believe God has ordered these steps for June. God says study to show yourself approved, so come step out in this deeper level of knowing. Should you want to know more about the timing of God and see things that are being prepared even now, you will enjoy this book. It may amaze and surprise you at how close we are to choosing the mark of the beast in our lives. After you read this book, you will choose no.

It is my prayer for you that you read this book and be aware of what the Word of God says about what June has written. She has given Biblical reference to everything she has talked about. I believe your eyes will be opened more about the timing of God in this matter after you delve into the depths of this book. Beware is the warning, be informed is the message, and be prepared is the word.

God bless you,

Theresa Jean Nichols,
Author of "To Know Me" Love Letters from God

This is one of the best books I have read on the subject of the mark of the beast. This book makes you aware that this is real. This is something that is here now, not in the future. When I first started reading on the subject years ago, it wasn't so real.

Over the last 40 years I have seen things come about to make this happen and it is here. This book will enlighten you to not be blind to this manipulation of the enemy and help you to be able to refuse the mark of the beast.

God says so many times in His word that He "would not have us to be ignorant" (Romans 1:13, 11:25; I Corinthians 10:1, 12:1; II Corinthians 1:8, 2:11; I Thessalonians 4:13; II Peter 3:8). Be wise to what the enemy has in the world that will I highly recommend this book to be added to any library.

A Must Read!

Wanda Jordan, Evangelist

ACKNOWLEDGMENTS

This book is an extension of the love and support of the spiritual mothers and fathers, prayer partners, and fellow ministers in my life. They teach me how to be a servant to the Body of Christ and how to trust in the Holy Spirit as my guide.

I want to thank my spiritual father, Pastor Rod Parsley, in whom I studied under at World Harvest Bible College (now Valor College). Your generosity to my family will forever be appreciated. Thank you for imparting into my family's life.

Thank you to my other spiritual parents, Dr. Christian and Robin Harfouche. The whole Harfouche family is a blessing! As I travel down the road to the doctorate degree, I'm learning tremendous amount of revelation. Thank you for following through on the vision of International Miracle Institute.

I especially want to thank my spiritual mother, Prophetess Melody Frazier Morris. She is a mighty woman of God and has been by my side through thick and thin. I learned about humility and forgiveness in a way that only God could show through her. Thank you.

I give all reverence and honor to Dr. Morris Cerullo for serving the Body of Christ for 68 years! I attended his 2015 World Conference and it changed my life! I received his special blessings! Thank you!

I also want to thank Pastor Greg Plummer and the congregation at Clarksville International Church for putting up with my rocky walk with Christ over the past 15 years and still loving me. Thank you Pastor Greg for investing in my family's life and sending us all to Bible College.

I want to thank Pastor Louis Montoya for showing me what real servant hood is like. His church reflects his heart.

Thank you to Pastor Todd Lackey for showing me how to bridge the Body of Christ together through love in spite of doctrine. You are a giant and I love Ms. Wendy too!

Thank you to Prophet Mark D. White for being like a spiritual father and rebuking and encouraging while steering me on the right path. I appreciate your wisdom.

I thank all the pastors in Clarksville, Tennessee. Our city is the Gateway to the World. We believe in missions and send missionaries out all over the world, along with our soldiers at Fort Campbell.

Thank you to Wanda Jordan for being such a loyal friend to my mother and helping us along life's path.

Thank you to Laurenda Whisenhunt who is a mighty woman of God and great example at being a woman. Period.

Thank you to Pastor Glenda Lockwood for being there for me through the thick and thin too.

Thank you to Evangelist Anthony Presswood and his beautiful wife, Heidi. Anthony is a revivalist and I believe God is going to use him mightily in the great awakening, which has already began!

Thank you to my other spiritual mother, Patricia Franklin Thomas for teaching me about trusting God for miracles.

Thank you to Theresa Nichols, and Joe'l Montgomery for your friendship.

Thank you especially to my children, in whom I am honored to be your mother. I love you and my grandchildren with all my heart.

Thank you to my brothers and sister. They have put up with a lot over the years. I love you!

Last but not least, a big thank you to my very best friend, Brenda Sue Bush. You are the greatest example of a Christian in my life and I love you with all my heart. There is nothing better than singing and dancing to Jesus! And, we can't leave out the baby dog Sweetie!

CHAPTERS

	Book Reviews	iv
	Acknowledgments	vi
1	Setting the Stage	Pg 1
2	My Theory	Pg 5
3	My Experience in London	Pg 9
4	A Global Tower of Babel	Pg 37
5	What is the chip/RFID tag?	Pg 39
6	Challenges of Selling to Christians	Pg 41
7	Marketing of the Ages	Pg 43
8	Agenda Setting Theory	Pg 49
9	Marketing The RFID: EU vs. USA	Pg 53
10	Spiritual Cost of the Mark	Pg 57
	References	Pg 59
	London Credits	Pg 63

SELLING THE MARK OF THE BEAST

SETTING THE STAGE

I must begin this book explaining the situation, which led up to the discovery of the human implantation chip and its imminent implementation. At this time I am in Graduate School at Austin Peay State University in Clarksville, TN. I am 43 years old and APSU sponsored my trip to London for a Study Abroad Class in Communications. My major is Corporate Communications and the Cooperative Center for Study Abroad (CCSA) offered a class in Public Relations for Winter 2011/2012. I was happy to represent my university during an epic point in history with the Queen's Jubilee Year in 2012 and the fact that London is hosting the 2012 London Olympics.

My trip lasted from December 26, 2011 to January 10, 2012. One other girl from APSU attended with me on this trip. While on the trip we traveled to many museums, parks, buildings, and participated in tours, etc. We visited such sites as Stonehenge and Bath, Buckingham Palace and other famous destinations. I was studying marketing and advertising. I had the honor of receiving training from the top three global marketing and advertising firms. As a class requirement, I had to pay attention to all forms of advertising and media and write about them daily. This caused me to quickly evaluate and adapt to their cultural mindset. I interviewed many Londoners and learned a lot.

However, the trip to the London Transport Museum on day three changed my life forever. The museum displayed an area called *Sense in the City*; which is about the future of technology. When I discovered the implementation of the Radio Frequency Identification Device (RFID) underneath human skin, it altered the course of my destiny. This discovery led to many hours of research and produced a research paper for graduate school.

The website describes *Sense in the City*, "A centre piece of the exhibition is an interactive table with eight screens that allows visitors to view a wealth of film, animations, data visualisations and images on subjects ranging from the cashless society and driverless cars to reactive buildings and augmented reality.

Visitors will be invited to join in and give their views about whether the plethora of new digital information and opportunity for access is exciting, a huge worry or a total waste of time". (LT Museum, 2012).

My research paper requirements in this class are to write a paper comparing a product and the marketing strategy differences in the United Kingdom versus the United States. The professors of my class were from the University of Kentucky in Louisville. Once I approached the professors with the interest of the RFID tags/chips, they allowed me to conduct research and gather sources outside of the normal academic boundaries. My professors were interested in hearing my perspective on this hot topic.

Normal college standards discourage and even disallow sources such as Fox News or basically any conservative Christian sources.

Now, back to the museum visit...While in the London Transport Museum in the *Sense in the City* section, goose bumps rose on my arms as I stood there gazing upon the reality of the implementation of the mark of the beast. Staring at me on the entrance to the section the sign said, "...in London over the next decade".

It shocked me. The Bible explains how we will not be able to buy or sell without this mark. (Revelation 13:17). Considering I previously attended World Harvest Bible College before and raised children that preached the gospel since childhood; I am very aware of this phenomenon. It quickly sobered me to the realities of the times we are living in.

This book is a reflection of my years' worth of research from 2012. I submitted this paper to two universities and now the Lord says it is time to present it to the world.

When I first came back from London, I wanted to warn the world and tell them what I discovered but after researching other people who previously went down this road and the backlash other Christians were receiving when they talked about the mark of the beast and the system, I backed out due to fear. However, three years later, the Holy Spirit is leading me, so thus, I am obeying Him.

As far as my personal life and the viewpoint from the research, I will share more about my life.

My education has been an uphill battle. I quit high school my junior year and married at 16 years old. A few years later I received my General Education Development (GED). I tried going to a community college a few years later but only lasted a year and a half. I became too bogged down with raising the three kids alone.

Years later, I attended Bible College at 36 years old for a little over a year. I was not able to graduate, then as a last attempt, when my last child was entering her senior year, I went to APSU to finish my bachelor's degree in public relations.

I finally achieved my lifelong dream at the age of 42! I graduated with a 3.54 GPA and formed two organizations on campus. The school offered to pay my graduate school and I became a Graduate Assistant.

During this time, I went to London and graduated early with a 3.74 GPA. My mentor and boss at the school offered to pay for my doctorate degree and become a professor. However, after praying about it the Lord told me not to accept the offer. Now I am currently in school to receive a doctorate in Theology through the International Miracle Institute under the direction of Dr. Christian Harfouche. I plan to graduate in August 2015.

Currently I started my own business and travel to preach. My heart is to share the love of Jesus with others and mainly in the prisons and nursing homes. Yes, I have encountered many obstacles to my walk with God and my education, but I never failed to continue trying. A true winner never quits. We keep pressing on.

With this information about my background, now you can obtain a better understanding to my interpretations of the world's events. The following chapters are the results of this research and experience.

MY THEORY

RFID (radio frequency identification device) technology is part of the marketing plan for the New World Order agenda. The Bible speaks about the end of days in which the world is under a one-world government and the Antichrist. Christians are aware this climactic ending is near, so we are well aware of the signs of our times.

The Bible says, "For we wrestle not against flesh and blood, but against principalities, against powers, against the rulers of the darkness of this world, against spiritual wickedness in high places." (Ephesians 6:12, KJV). There is a spirit in the world that we call the god of this world. This spirit is what we term as worldly, or the spirit of antichrist. This spirit is in direct opposition to the kingdom of heaven. It is the kingdom of this world (spirit of antichrist or worldly spirit) versus the kingdom of heaven.

> *1 John 4:2-6 ESV says, "By this you know the Spirit of God: every spirit that confesses that Jesus Christ has come in the flesh is from God, and every spirit that does not confess Jesus is not from God. This is the spirit of the antichrist, which you heard was coming and now is in the world already. Little children, you are from God and have overcome them, for he who is in you is greater than he who is in the world. They are from the world; therefore they speak from the world, and the world listens to them. We are from God. Whoever knows God listens to us; whoever is not from God does not listen to us. By this we know the Spirit of truth and the spirit of error."*

We only have two choices as a human. We can either live to please the spirit of antichrist, which pleases the appetites of the flesh, or we live to please the Holy Spirit, which denies the appetites of the flesh and surrenders to God's will instead. The chip will force you to choose.

If we choose the side of the kingdom of Heaven, we will be greatly persecuted and treated as an alien on this Earth. "Dear friends, I urge you, as foreigners and exiles, to abstain from sinful desires, which wage war against your soul" (2 Peter 2:11, NIV).

Growing numbers of people believe there is a group called the Illuminati, which is a secret society and they control the world. This group operates under the kingdom of the world, antichrist spirit. As far as we know, this group began in the late 1700s. This NWO marketing plan is the ultimate marketing plan of the ages. If my research is correct, this plan spans across two centuries of dynamics controlled by a secret society group of intellectual thinkers called the Illuminati. This group effectively plans to control the world through finance, education, marketplace, religion, and humans.

This take-over plan includes the communications theory - Agenda Setting Theory. This theory suggests that a group or force controls our media. I will explain more about this later on in the book. The ultimate marketing plan involves a strategy to effectively change the course of events for the whole world. This group owns the media and controls our content.

I will examine RFID as the end-means plan of this group to deliver the goal of the one-world government. RFID implantation into the skin of humans will be used to track human's every move, monitor vital signs, interact with technology such as opening the door to your house, and ultimately be the next smart card to access your finances. Citizens will not be able to buy or sell without this chip; or as the Christians call it, the mark of the beast. Marketers will be challenged in convincing Christians to participate in this scheme. The Bible speaks of a one-world government, so the Christians feel warned against this plot. It is a plan of the future Antichrist.

The best way to convince society to accept this mark and participate in the world's system is to infiltrate all areas of society. Change the music, textbooks for the youth so they grow up with the world's vision, change the television shows that feed the mind constantly, change the news so it reflects the agenda, etc.

A great reflection of this truth is through symbols. Symbols reflect ideologies and are meant to trigger feelings and thoughts. When you see a cross what is the first thing that pops in your mind? An upside down cross? A circle with a line through it? So many events in the mainstream media contain the same symbols. This reflects the spirit behind the event.

The 2012 Olympics in London was loaded with triangles and various Illuminati symbols. In the opening ceremony, they gave homage to the invention of the internet and practically worshipped it. In addition, they displayed horror figures chasing children around. The whole presentation was strange. I understand they were attempting to share their culture with the world, but it came across as the way I experienced it while there. It was very materialistic, the supremacy was with the government with socialized health care, and soul-less.

It's hard to explain except that one day I was on the business side of town and was shocked watching the business people walk down the street. They looked like dead-men walking with no expressions on their faces, blank-looks, and empty. It was so odd that I sat my camera on the table at the bistro and recorded it.

Going back to symbols and society, please check out the music industry; those videos are loaded with the same type of symbols. Also, investigate awards shows, etc. It has infiltrated all of mainstream society. There are many books out there that delve into this spirit of antichrist, or as some call it, Luciferianism. Please investigate it for yourself.

Before I am accused of being a conspiracy theorist, please consider that prior to my trip to London, I avoided these topics due to my other passionate endeavors in college. The discovery in Europe affected my life and opened my eyes to the truth.

This event set me on a course to investigate and research the global plan to chip all humans, products, infrastructure, and the whole planet's animals. It is all much bigger than we can ever imagine.

Disclaimer: I am not here to change your theology about pre-tribulation rapture, mid-tribulation rapture, post-tribulation rapture or no rapture. I am merely explaining the facts I discovered and leave the decision up to you on how to best react to the information. God bless you and I pray for every person reading this book for clear discernment from the Holy Spirit.

MY EXPERIENCE IN LONDON

My class assignments required me to travel over Europe and write about my experience on a daily basis. The professors provoked questions and thoughts to consider about advertising, marketing, and the media all around us. It caused us to look at everything and decipher it according to hidden messages, etc.

We examined things like how advertisements were displayed on objects, buildings, people, etc. We also considered the surroundings (environment surrounding advertisements), the mediums used, the color schemes, the symbols, etc. It all works together. Colors have significance along with shapes. So, it alerts our minds to certain feelings those designs may provoke.

We also critiqued the museums we visited. In this chapter I will examine the museums according to my theory of the new world order agenda trying to brainwash society to believe their doctrine. I will explain the exhibits, signs and messages behind such displays.

LONDON TRANSPORT MUSEUM

Sense in the City Exhibit – This exhibit displayed the advancement of technology such as the old phones, typewriters, computers, etc., and displayed the integration within the smartphone. The smartphone incorporates all of that technology into one place.

The most intriguing thing to me was the section on the RFID chip. I previously was aware of this technology and to see it in this museum was amazing. The RFID will be the technology that the new world order will use to mark the citizens on Earth with the mark of the beast as told in the book of Revelations in the Bible.

This exhibit of the RFID chip is to show the world how this will be used soon to identify humans, as it is already used in animals and products. Christians will not allow the government to put the chip in their skins, as they believe this is the mark of the beast and will be doomed to Hell if they accept the worldly system.

The sign for *Sense in the City* says, "Smart, connected and on the move." "Powerful new forces are shaping the way we live, work and travel in the city. GPS, electric vehicles, pervasive wireless, sensing, near field communication, multi-touch surfaces, open data, smartphones and a blizzard of new apps are combining to redefine the way we see and experience London.

Sense and the City unravels the digital future and illustrates the power of emerging applications and poses questions about mobility, society and work in London over the next decade."

Another wall painted says Information Transforms the City – "Changing access to information – how we acquire, process and use it – alters and renews our experience of the city. Newspapers, telephones, computers and the internet have each driven massive changes in how we work, relax and socialize, and how we understand the city itself."

The next sign says, Cities of the Future, "We journey into the future filled with trepidation and excitement. We imagine the worlds to come in the hope of bringing about change, stimulating new ideas, gaining a competitive edge, or better understanding the present. We explore social, philosophical, architectural and technological ideas to create cities we will never see."

	Exhibits About Changing Technologies
Conversations in the City	*"Having a chat, doing serious business, or responding to an emergency, all become easier with the growth of telephone networks."* In the case is old dial-up phones, operated-assisted phones and older cell phones. **120 years ago** – Telephones become indispensable for businesses but all calls must be routed by a human switchboard operator. Initially only used for serious conversations, switchboard operators interrupt any conversation they considered too frivolous. **63 years ago** – Full automation of the UK telephone network begins. By 1978, you can call anywhere in the UK without going through a human operator.

Conversations in the City Cont'd	**26 years ago** – Two Vodafone employees make the first mobile phone call in the UK. New generations of phones follow, adding text messaging in 1991 and internet access in 2000.
Shopping in the City	*"New technologies change our access to money and the ease with which we spend it. Critics argue that money became too easy to spend prior to the financial crisis like the South Sea Bubble of 1720, the Dot Com Bubble of 2000 and more recent financial difficulties."* In the case is a poster that says, "You can shop without cash with a Barclaycard (credit card). Then coins, eBay for Dummies book, eBay coffee mug, calculator/adding machine." **2100 years ago** – The first coins in Britain minted by Celtic tribes. We have to wait until 1694 for the Bank of England to issue the first bank notes. Over the years, water marks, metal threads, holograms and ultraviolet printing are added to prove authenticity and to prevent forgeries. **45 years ago** – Barclaycard launch the first credit card in the UK. A magnetic strip on the back holds account information. From 2004, UK credit cards contain a data chip which must be verified with the holder's PIN. **16 years ago** – Ebay founded by computer programmer Pierre Omidyar. A trusted digital payment method is essential to Ebay's success so it acquires PayPal in 2002. Today there are over 10 million items for sale on the UK site at any one time. **3 years ago** – Barclaycard produces a contactless payment terminal enabling fast transactions for items worth $15 or less. A contactless payment card is held close to the reader, and the amount is deducted from the customer's account without the need for a PIN. Could this be the start of a cashless society?

Breaking News in the City	*"New technologies bring wider coverage and faster dissemination of news to greater numbers of people."* In the case is an old dial radio, a walkie-talkie device, and old newspapers. **300 years ago** – Newspapers proliferate as the government relaxes controls and duties on printing and paper. Hundreds of newspapers end up covering news from all points of view. **75 years ago** – Millions tune in nightly during the momentous events of the mid 20th century. From the 1960s, portable transistor radios take radio out of the home. **25 years ago** – The Sony Watchman is an early attempt to provide rich media on the move. Television has taken over from radio as the main source of news for most people decades ago, but lacks the portability of transistor radios.
Entertaining in the City	*"Where there is information there can also be entertainment new technologies bring entertainment to wider audiences."* In the case is two books, "The New Machiavelli", Atari Game Boy and games, and the old Atari Video Game Console. **76 years ago** – Penguin paperbacks are published for the first time. These light-weight, easy-to-carry books prove instantly popular and satisfy reader's desire to enjoy good books anywhere anytime. **25 years ago** – Atari 2600 video games console proves massively popular during the 1980s, bringing arcade style digital entertainment into your living room. **15 years ago** – Nintendo Gameboy provides digital gaming on the move, as long as the AA batteries last out in these days before the integral rechargeable power pack.

Socialising in the City	*"Eating, drinking, debating, doing business, music, dancing, flirting, formenting political unrest. By 2000, digital locations are as important as physical locations for socializing."* In the case is teacups on saucers, magazine, teapot, and college Harvard University t-shirt. **300 years ago** – Coffee houses become popular across London serving the exotic new drink. They become centres for philosophical, political and artistic debate as well as venues for doing business. Lloyd's of London the insurance company was founded in Lloyd's coffee shop. **55 years ago** – Italian coffee bars are the essential place for teenagers to hang out in the 1950s and 1960s, providing juke box music and a hip, European vibe. **35 years ago** – TimeOut is the essential guide to London, listing at various times music, theatre, dance, cinema, sport, bars, cafes, restaurants and 'agit prop' – agitation and propaganda. **7 years ago** – Mark Zuckerberg founds Facebook at Harvard University. Within 5 years Facebook moves off campus to become the most popular social networking site on the planet. Users meet, chat, flirt and also set up groups for specialists interests, political campaigns and products.
Transmitting Information in the City	*"Moving electronic information has required specialist equipment but in the 21st century, most of us do it every day using mobile phones and the internet."* In the case is computer floppy disks and other items. **120 years ago** – Morse code keys send information as dots and dashes down telegraph cables that encircle the world, creating 'the Victorian internet'. Information including war news and stock prices takes just minutes to reach London from around the globe.

Transmitting Information in the City Cont'd	**90 years ago** – Canisters carrying documents are moved using air pressure through 120 kilometres of tubes under London. Pneumatic tube systems continue into the 21st century, carrying documents, cash, medical samples and components. **Around 45 years ago** – Type balls are the printing heads of some Teletype machines forming part of the Telex network, enabling organisations to send information electronically around the world. **35 years ago** – Acoustically-coupled modems connect computers over telephone lines to access bulletin boards, forerunners of internet forums. During the 1980s, companies lay fibre optic cables, increasing the capacity of the telephone network in preparation for digital services. **40 years ago** – 8-inch disks begin to replace punched tape for storing digital information. 5% and 3 ½ inch disks appear in the 1970s and 80s with optical discs in the 1990s. In 2010, a USB stick can hold more data than 8 billion kilometres of punched tape.
Computing Power in the City	*"Our ability to do interesting things with increasingly large amounts of information moves from the 1950s laboratory to the 1980s living room, and into our pockets in the 2000s."* In the case is an old Sinclair computer keyboard, cassette recorder, calculators, and a big keyboard. **35 years ago** – Programmable calculators are cheap and small enough that people can buy their own personal piece of computing equipment. No games though. **25 years ago** – The Commodore 64 computer becomes the world's best selling personal computer of all time. A record of it continues holds into the 21st century. For many people, the Commodore 64 is the first computer they have at home. **25 years ago** – The ZX Spectrum enters many British homes as a competitor to the US Commodore 64. The UK computer software industry establishes itself to fulfill demand for games and other programs.

Recording in the City	*"Evolving technologies enable increasing numbers of us to record our sense of the city while CCTV records us all."* In the case is a CCTV camera, Polaroid camera and other digital cameras with pictures. <u>**55 years ago**</u> – Browne cameras have transformed photography from an expensive, technical art form and turn it into a medium almost anyone can afford. <u>**35 years ago**</u> – Polaroid cameras herald instant image making. Film is no longer sent to laboratories for processing and amateur photographers make full use of this new privacy. <u>**15 years ago**</u> – CCTV cameras make Britons allegedly the most watched people on the planet, raising questions about the relative benefits of large scale surveillance.
Time and Space in the City	*"Our sense of time and its importance in the city changes over the centuries, just as new transport modes and routes bring far-flung places close together."* In the case is a pocket-watch, wrist-watches, London A-Z Street Atlas, Central Line Timetables British Rail Book, TimeTables from Southern Electric Book, Local Road & Rail Timetable business card, little black-books, calendar appointment book and maps. <u>**80 years ago**</u> – Diaries have changed from narrative records of the pasto to lists of appointments to be kept in the future. <u>**120 years ago**</u> – Tickets become a ubiquitous necessity for travel on the London bus and growing underground rail networks. Paper tickets decline with the introduction of the Oyster Card for contactless payment in 2003. <u>**120 years ago**</u> – Timetables are essential for running the railway system and ensure that the time is precisely the same across the city.
Time and	

Space in the City Cont'd	**120 years ago** – Pocket watches are carried by most business people to ensure that they are on time around the city. Cheap digital watches hit the market in the 1980s, giving everyone access to split second accuracy. **75 years ago** – A to Z maps redefine how Londoners think of their city. For the first time it is easy to find addresses in neighbourhoods you don't know.
Today	*"Smartphones provide access to a whole range of activities, products and services in the city that were previously tied to fixed locations and wired-in equipment."* In the case is two smartphones. • Voice, video, email and messenger conversations anywhere • Photography and video capture and upload with location information attached instantly • Video downloads • Shared diaries on the go • Payments made through PayPal and credit card reader apps • Barcode picture message tickets • Route planning, timetable and live travel information apps • Individual and communal games • Streamed or saved music • 24/7 access to billions of people and millions of special interests through hundreds of social networks • Instant location information

Next wall painting is, The Future is Nearly Now – "We are promised lifetimes worth of entertainment, information, shopping and socializing, instantly available through phones, computers and smart gadgets. This saturated digital connectivity fulfils many futurist dreams, transcending the clunky architectures and technologies of the past to define the future for our age.

Following that painting is various pictures of movies depicting the future such as *The Fifth Element*, which features a towering city and flying cars. Also featured is the movie *Mother of Storms*. It depicts the apocalyptic ending with disease, climate change, etc.

Next sign – "The city of the future is a character in itself, facilitating endless dramatic narratives. The dysfunctional, dystopian city in these stories reveals many of our preoccupations and fears in the very real cities of today."

Dystopia means a bad society or like an oppressed people/society. That sign is speaking against the Christians who would be against this technology because of the Bible prophetic unfolding of the end of days. Notice how it says we may have fears and preoccupations.

Next sign – Expanding Digital Language – More than 14 new words appear in the English Language every day. This wall endeavours to explain some words and phrases that have recently come into common usage in the mushrooming field of digital technology.

In June 2009, web 2.0 became the millionth English word. Source: Global Language Monitor".

Definitions of Digital Language

Avatar	A graphic representation of someone in cyberspace. An avatar can take the form of a photograph, cartoon or a three dimensional animation. Origins: Derived from the Hindu word for a spirit in human form. First used in computer games in the 1980s.
Web 2.0	Recent developments on the World Wide Web allowing more dynamic content including user interaction, user generated content, and social networking. Origins: Coined in 1999 with reference to numbered computer software releases by Darcy DiNucci in her article Fragmented Future.
Web 3.0	Possible future developments of the World Wide Web. These could include greater personalization as well as the ability for machines to better understand the meaning of digital information.
RFID (radio-frequency identification)	A technology for transferring small amounts of information to and from tags over short distances. Tags can be attached to products, crates, animals or people. Each tag contains a microchip and an antenna to communicate with a reader. Origins: The first patent to use the abbreviation RFID was granted to Charles Walton in 1983.

The next sign, "The rise of digital technology will create a society that is...31% POLARISED, 18% UNFAIR, 31% FAIR, 20% CLASSLESS." At the bottom of the poster it reads, "So 64% of you think that the rise of digital technology will create a society that is fair or classless. Compared with 36% of you that think it will make it polarized or unfair." These statistics are to give the impression that the world is in line with the technology advances they are portraying in the exhibit. RFID tagging of humans is one of those advances.

The next section is Visions of Tomorrow. The sign says, "London's Royal College of Art (RCA) is unique – a global centre of excellence where tomorrow's top designers perfect their vision for a fast-changing world.

Here the RCA presents a practical picture of the near future with today's technology on tomorrow's streets. This is how we may move and communicate in 2020."

- **London E-motion** vehicle – "London E-motion is an urban, electrically powered scooter, for public use. The E-motion performs as an extension to the driver's body expressions and mood. Using large visible communication surfaces, the E-Motion improves communications between all road users."
- **Senseable Bus** – "The Senseable Bus aims to bring moving transport and cultural information to the street. The idea is that buses in 2020 will sense the city and visually react to their environment, in order to show different kinds of live data. They will be covered with OLED light displays, so they can change their skin to show different content."
- **Urban Flower** – "The car is over 100 years old and is not effective in a large, crowded modern city. Our current system of traffic control is also under pressure. This concept enables a fresh start by removing lanes, traffic lights, zebra crossings and the car itself. In their place, the UrbanFlower will be a vehicle that is available to everyone, respects humans, and even behaves like them by navigating the streets in the same way people move on a crowded pavement."
- **The Window** by Leena Kangaskoski and Ana Minguez – "The aim of tis proposal is to create a system using existing equipment to encourage interaction and transparency within the London Underground network. We decided to transform the obtrusive presence of CCTV surveillance into an interactive action. The system allows passengers to have information about their location above and below

ground as if through a 'window' as well as allowing them to interact with other passengers."
- **The Climate Machine** – "The Climate Machine responds dynamically to transport use in London and visualizes it using a wall of light bulbs. The Climate Machine not only visualizes data, but also acts as an icon of change towards a future where we are fully accountable for our energy use."
- **Augmented Wayfinding** by Michael Lum – "Every person has a unique understanding of their surroundings and how it will affect their travel within the city. However, while on the street this information largely remains with the individual. This system proposes to integrate touchscreens, augmented reality displays, dynamically updated content, and social networks into the signage found on the streets of London."
- **Discover Your Borough** by Alice Moloney – "Discover your Borough is a wayfinding system for pedestrians. On a small scale and hand-drawn, the system is to be experienced at a slower pace. The signage is placed above and below eye level to encourage a sense of discovery and curiosity in navigation. It was inspired by the village of Chrora on the island of Serios, Greece."
- **Youvenirs** by Jaakko Tuomivaara – "Youvenirs provide a way of both keeping and sharing your travels in the digital age. It utilizes the data gathered about your journeys on the Oyster card and gives it back to you in a personalized, visually interesting and easily understandable form. This can be shared quickly and easily through email, Facebook and other social media."

Then we see other boards and this one says The Internet of Things – "*The Internet of Things* is about giving each individual physical object a representation in the digital world.

This may done by attaching radio communications to each object, such as RFID tags, or by attaching QR and bar codes.

The Internet of Things is providing increasing volumes of environmental and position data as well as interactivity and autonomous action for a diverse range of products, devices, vehicles and buildings."

Payment by Mobile Phone – "RFID chips embedded in mobile phones enable them to operate as credit cards and electronic cash."

Implanted RFID Tag – "The RFID chips that facilitate electronic payment systems can be implanted under the skin. This method of identification and payment is already popular at some beach clubs where clothing with pockets is not the norm. As RFID readers proliferate for a variety of purposes, someone with sufficient resources and knowledge could use your implanted tag to identify and track you in real time."

Mobile Cell Location – "Each mobile phone base-station serves a particular cell. As we carry mobile devices around, they automatically communicate with several of the closest base stations. Interpreting the signals to these base-stations can provide real time location and tracking down to about 50 metres in a city. Networks also record this information.

These records are kept private by the mobile phone companies. There have been discussions in the UK and elsewhere about how long it is appropriate for companies to retain this data."

How GPS Works – "The GPS (Global Positioning System) uses a network of around 30 satellites, each transmitting precise position and time information. A GPS receiver picks up signals from three or more of these satellites and uses the time taken for the signal to reach the device from the satellites to work out its precise position on Earth."

At the end of the exhibit is a painting on the wall, "By occupying the urban landscape, we define it and transform it. The buildings and businesses come and go; the people remain. The real digital cities are made of us - Owen Thomas – mashable.com"

LONDON SCIENCE MUSEUM

In the one of the displays is a big camera on the top of the wall (big brother watching)...the sign within this display says, "Developments in electronic technology allowed the observation and analysis of a broad range of everyday actions carried out by the public, from walking down the street to using a telephone. The rise of surveillance was consistent with the increasing acceptance of the flow of information as a normal, even essential, aspect of life. Many people felt that the benefits of information-gathering in this way, such as crime prevention and personal convenience, outweighed the disadvantages, such as loss of privacy and personal liberty."

Also on the picture about surveillance it says, "By 1999 some 250 million was spent annually in the UK on closed-circuit television (CCTV) surveillance systems involving an estimated 300,000 cameras introduced to reduce street crimes such as burglary and mugging, the cameras prompted concerns from civil liberties and crime prevention organizations. – Owen Thomas, mashable.com."

Please notice how they try to justify having cameras everywhere. They said, "..a normal, even essential aspect of life." They want society to adapt to the government prying into your personal life. Not only are there cameras everywhere in Europe, but big microphones as well such as on the outside of buildings on the streets!

Another area displayed information about drones (spyplanes). The museum displayed graphics in which they answered questions. Here are a few examples:

Have unmanned drones been in use long? "The military have used drones for decades, although the number has really increased in the past ten years. Ninety-nine percent of aerial drones are military, so this is where all the research funding comes from. Recently, the police have started to use them as a cheap alternative to manned helicopters. Drones are used by the military to spy in places where it is too dangerous to send manned aircraft."

Why let drones fly above us? "The law is very strict. If the police want to fly a drone they have to get special permission from air traffic control and they are not allowed to fly it over busy areas. The person operating the drone has to be in direct control and keep sight of it at all times. This restricts how useful drones can be, but there is a lot of pressure building to change the law. Researchers aim to make safer, smarter drones that can detect and avoid aircraft, buildings, and other obstacles."

Following is a display with a picture of a HexRotor. It's a cool-looking drone with many arms and small.

What is a HexRotor? Display reads, "We've installed a minicomputer that sends signals to each of the HexRotor's six motors and this enables it to fly. It also has a positioning system linked to the computer. This means we can tell it to follow a certain route on a map and takeoff and land automatically. In the future aerial drones will be intelligent enough to fly with almost no human supervision."

Why use aerial drones in towns and cities? "Drones can be better than helicopters for surveillance because they're cheaper to buy, fly and maintain. You don't need a highly trained pilot either. A few police forces around the UK have just begun to use the drones and they're keen to use more of them in the future. Merseyside, Staffordshire and Essex police have all started testing aerial drones in recent years."

When will HexRotor take to the skies? "We first flew HexRotor in November 2009 and so far we haven't had any crashes! In two years we hope to sell it for use in police surveillance, or possibly the military. Another option we're exploring is using HexRotor in the nuclear power industry to inspect areas with dangerous radiation levels. In the US, flying drones are used to police the border with Mexico."

What Makes HexRotor Ideal for Towns and Cities? "HexRotor can fly up close to buildings with amazing precision. It's six rotors let it hover motionlessly to peer into a window, which is no mean feat in the gusty conditions you get in towns and cities. It can also fly at an angle to squeeze down a narrow alleyway. Drones like HexRotor can peer into windows without anyone noticing, and can even fly around inside a building."

Please notice how they try to explain this invasion as "Drones are used by the military to spy in places where it is too dangerous to send manned aircraft." Yes, we want to protect our service members, but we also know where this technology will be used in the future!

The Listening Post Exhibit - On the sign as a Disclaimer it said, "*Listening Post* features uncensored fragments of text from live chatroom data. It may occasionally include content that is unsuitable for children or which some visitors may find offensive. The material is not produced or solicited by the Science Museum, so the Museum is unable to accept responsibility for the nature of the content that the work may extract from these sources."

I filmed the event and posted on YouTube when I returned from London. I will also have this on my website, http://www.norfidchip.com

Then, before you listened to the conversation, on the inside wall it wrote, "*Listening Post* is a 'dynamic portrait' of online communication, displaying uncensored fragments of text, sampled in real-time, from public internet chatrooms and bulletin boards. Artists Mark Hansen and Ben Rubin have divided their work into seven separate 'scenes' akin to movements in a symphony. Each scene has its own 'internal logic', sifting, filtering and ordering the text fragments in different ways.

Listening Post is an extraordinary investigation into the character of online communication and the meaning of malleability of statistics. It is a recognized masterpiece of electronic and contemporary art, but Hansen and Rubin's use of media technologies and sophisticated data analysis techniques differentiates it from traditional visual art. It relies not only on materials and the built environment, but also on text data quoted from thousands of unwitting contributors' postings.

As *Listening Post* carries out its eavesdropping cycles and displays its findings to us, it implicates us in its voyeuristic activities. But we also experience a great sense of the humanity behind the data. Hansen and Rubin have almost created a modern-day oracle, a snapshot of the internet as we know it today and a monument to the ways we find to connect with each other and express our identities online. – Hannah Redler – Head of Science Museum Arts Projects."

The *Listening Post* displayed words or text as we listened to the various voices on Earth talking online. It was rather eerie knowing we were prying in on people's private conversations.

I sat there thinking, "Wonder what the powers-at-large are doing with all this data they're gathering? They are literally combining this data for future use and I'm sure it's not for our good."

This exhibit is scary because it gives the impression to the viewers that big brother is watching our every move on the internet. I do not believe this would be accepted in the United States because we are wearier of big brother than England. In England's culture, they are used to cameras being everywhere and speakers listening to conversations. The privacy issues this raises is that we are not private in our conversations on the internet. I understand things we post on Facebook if it is public, but if we are on our private page, noone should be able to watch it (although I know it is Facebook's property of all the material we load on their website). This presentation is eye-opening.

Electroboutique Pop-up Exhibit is about various arts meant to depict the media's impact on our culture. It was very bazaar. I will post all of the pictures on the www.norfidchip.com website as well.

I love this artwork because it shows a dog using his paw to play on a big iPad. The dog represents citizens/consumers being like puppets with the current technology such as the iPad. This is an animated artwork with the dog moving to work the iPad. This represents consumerism in that we try to download so many apps...we are obsessed with it. Also, it represents media control in that they use this technology to use us like puppets.

Another piece of artwork is s-shaped glass objects which look one way, but when you shine a light behind it you see the hidden message within. This artwork is unique in that it the only way to expose the language underneath is to shine a camera's light in to it. This reminds me of hidden cameras and big brother watching us. This reminds me of technological progress and design aspiration.

The two exhibits about big brother invading our privacy. send a message to the patrons that the big brother invasion is inevitable and OK.

IMPERIAL WAR MUSEUM

As you travel through the museum, we come to a sign, "Age of Ambivalence, 1960-2000. By the end of the twentieth century, the industrialised world had come to view poverty, famine and disease not as inevitable features of society, but as conditions which could be solved by technology. Yet as the pace of technological change accelerated in the late twentieth century, industrialised societies entered an age of ambivalence – of mixed feelings about technology and its role in the world. As advanced technologies affected more aspects of everyday life, anxieties about their side effects and unintended consequences undermined popular trust in the concept of progress and its promoters.

There were numerous examples of the uneasy relationship between technology and society. The new biological sciences, exploring the genetic code in the laboratory, offered up frightening scenarios in which adult animals were cloned, sheep could be engineered to express human medicine in their milk, and the practical processes for such procedures could be taught in the classroom.

Car use rose dramatically and showed no sign of abating, despite the crippling congestion in towns and the continuing death toll from traffic accidents. And, as powerful computers pervaded every aspect of life, so they offered powerful tools for surveillance and social control.

The artefacts displayed here are symbols of ambivalence. This is neither utopia nor dystopia. It is the modern world."

World War II Exhibit. In an effort to explain history, one sign relays, "The Christian Churches – Antisemitism as an organized idea originated in the rivalry between the Christian and Jewish religions in the Roman Empire. For many centuries, Christians were taught to regard the Jews as evil, and such beliefs persisted into the 20th century.

The Christian churches generally opposed the Nazis' anti-Semitism, but tended to agree that 'Jewish influence' was undesirable. They rarely felt responsible for defending Jews, apart from converts to their own denominations. In 1937 the Pope denounced Nazi racial ideas, but not anti-Jewish laws."

A video plays about the history of Hitler in the Imperial War Museum and it is obvious that it is sending a message to society that Christians are to blame for Hitler killing the Jews in WWII. Although Hitler claims to use the Christian religion as the basis for his evil deeds, it is not the true Christian religion that drove the mass murders. This video does not reflect the true Christian faith. This is a message to turn society against the Christian faith. I have this video on the website as well.

Another display – **Antisemitism from ancient times** – "Antisemitism – 'the longest hatred' – developed over nearly 2,000 years, as Europe found ways to blame the Jews for more and more of society's ills. The Jews have often been the victims of massacres and other forms of persecution.

70AD, the destruction of the Temple in Jerusalem, the centre of the Jewish religion, by the Emperor Titus. Christians, then still a Jewish sub-sect, take this as a sign that God has rejected the other Jews.

1096, The First Crusade begins. A third of the Jewish population of Germany and Northern France is killed by crusaders on their way to the Holy Land.

1144, The first known 'blood libel'. Jews in Norwich are falsely accused of killing a Christian boy for ritual purposes. This superstition spreads throughout Europe, and will still be believed in the twentieth century. Part of the libel is the belief that Jewish leaders gather each year to select a victim. This starts the idea of a sinister Jewish conspiracy.

1215, The fourth Lateran Council under Pope Innocent III introduces a 'sign', usually a round yellow badge, which the Jews had to wear. The colour symbolizes penitence and shame.

1290, England expels its Jews, who are not readmitted until 1655.

1348, The Black Death. Jews are accused of causing the plague by poisoning wells and are massacred in many parts of Europe.

1492, The Jewish community of Spain, the world's largest, is forced to choose between conversion to Christianity or expulsion. Those who leave settle mainly in the Mediterranean world.

c.**1500**, The Jewish community of the Commonwealth of Poland and Lithuania becomes the largest in the world. Jews are drawn there by liberal laws and economic freedom.

1516, A district called 'The Ghetto' is established in Venice. Such walled areas to which Jews have been confined have existed for several centuries, but soon most German and Italian towns will force Jews to live in them.

1543, Martin Luther – founder of German Protestantism – publishes 'About the Jews and their Lies'. Luther turned strongly against the Jews when he failed to convert them.

1648-59, War and unrest in Poland-Lithuania result in large-scaled massacres of Jews. There is a new atmosphere of tolerance in Western Europe, which is beginning to readmit them.

1791, French Jews gain equal civic rights after the Revolution.

1772-95, Poland-Lithuania is partitioned between Russia, Prussia and Austria. Most Jews find themselves in the Russian Empire, which has hitherto excluded Jews.

1858, Lionel Rothschild takes his seat as the first Jewish Member of the British Parliament, previously closed to Jews.

1871, Unification of Germany, Jews gain equal rights throughout the new state.

1879, German journalist Wilhelm Marr coins the term 'antisemitism' and forms the Antisemitic League. This marks the beginning of anti-Semitism as a political movement, based on the notion of a Jewish 'race'.

1881, Russian Tsar Alexander II is a assassinated by revolutionary terrorists. Widespread pogroms (anti-Jewish riots) follow, triggering mass Jewish emigration to the US and Western Europe. Jews will often be blamed for socialist and revolutionary activities.

1894, Captain Alfred Dreyfus, the first Jew on the French Army's General Staff, is convicted of spying. When it is proved that senior officers have forged the evidence against him, a ten-year scandal – 'the Dreyfus affair' – breaks out. The 'anti-Dreyfusards' use anti-Semitic propaganda and sometimes violence.

1918-21, Pogroms in areas of Ukraine, Poland, Western Russia, Hungary, Slovakia and Romania. At least 60,000 Jews are killed.

Antisemitism in the early twentieth century – "Most European Jews lived in Eastern Europe, where anti-Semitism often took the form of violent riots called pogroms. Waves of pogroms struck the Russian Empire in 1903-1907 and again in 1919-1921, killing tens of thousands of Jews. Later Hungary, Romania and Poland passed anti-Jewish laws.

Antisemitic movements flourished in most countries. Riots had accompanied the Dreyfus affair in France. In Britain, famous writers such as Rudyard Kipling, G K Chesterton and T S Eliot expressed anti-Jewish prejudices. In the 1930s, Sir Oswald Mosley's British Union of Fascists carried out violent attacks on Jews."

Another display about World War II is **Propaganda and race hatred** – Propaganda, spread by modern means of communication, was one of the keys to Nazi success.

Through lurid images and simple messages repeated over and over again, Hitler and his propaganda minister, Joseph Goebbels, aroused and mobilized the masses.

The Nazis censored and then seized control of all the media. Radio, films, rallies, exhibitions and posters spread Nazi doctrines, especially anti-Semitism and racism. Children's books and school lessons were designed to incite the young to hate Jews. Throughout Germany signs were put up forbidding Jews to enter inns, restaurants, parks and even entire villages. Jews and 'Aryans' who associated with them, were often humiliated in public.

Top: Volksemptanger (People's Receiver). This inexpensive radio set brought speeches of Hitler and Goebbels to nearly every German home, but could receive short wave foreign broadcasts. Nazi propaganda programmes could also be heard over street loudspeakers, or at work, where listening in organised groups was often compulsory. The poster announces, 'All Germany listens to the Father on the People's Receiver.' Far right: The anti-Semitic exhibition 'The Eternal Jew' was opened by Goebbels at the German Museum, Munich, in November 1937, the displays included photographs and models of 'racially typical' Jewish features."

The Nuremberg Laws, From the Reich Law Gazette 1935 –

Reich Citizenship Law
ONLY A GERMAN OF PURE BLOOD CAN BE A CITIZEN.

For the Protection of German Blood and German Honour
MARRIAGES BETWEEN GERMANS OF PURE BLOOD AND JEWS ARE FORBIDDEN

JEWS ARE FORBIDDEN TO EMPLOY FEMALE SERVANTS UNDER THE AGE OF FORTY-FIVE

RELATIONS OUTSIDE OF MARRIAGE BETWEEN GERMANS OF PURE BLOOD AND JEWS ARE FORBIDDEN

JEWS ARE FORBIDDEN TO FLY THE SWASTIKA NATIONAL FLAG

THE PENALTY FOR BREAKING THESE LAWS IS IMPRISONMENT
First Regulation
To the Reich Citizenship Law

A JEW IS A PERSON DESCENDED FROM AT LEAST THREE GRANDPARENTS WHO ARE FULL JEWS BY RACE. A 'MISCHLING' (PERSON OF JEWISH DESCENT)…IS ALSO CONSIDERED A JEW IF HE IS DESCENDED FROM TWO JEWISH GRANDPARENTS (AND IS)…A MEMBER OF THE JEWISH RELIGIOUS COMMUNITY….(OR) MARRIED TO A JEW (OR VARIOUS OTHER QUALIFICATIONS).

On the wall in this area it says,
"This struggle is one of ideologies and racial differences and will have to be conducted with unprecedented unmerciful and unrelenting harshness – Adolf Hitler."

TATE MODERN MUSEUM

I Decided Not to Save the World Exhibit. The sign says, "Curious acts and seemingly small gestures unite the works in this exhibition. Artists Mounira Al Solh, Yto Barrada, Mircea Cantor and the collective Slavs and Tatars devise playful interventions into their everyday environments, combining social comment and investigation with humour or irony to throw off our habits of thinking. Emerging from the specific contexts in which they are made, the light-hearted approach of these works belies the artists' acute socio-political insights.

The title of the exhibition is taken from Mircea Cantor's 2011 video of the same name in which a single take of a child saying 'I decided not to save the world' is shown in a continuous loop. The work is emblematic of the complexity that underlies the simplest of statements and is typical of the way Cantor responds to contemporary concerns using simple and direct gestures."

Yto Barrada is known for the playful nature of her work, rooted in the specific context of Tangier, Morocco, where she lives and works. Her sculpture, poster series and film included in this exhibition use humour and satire to address the country's rapid modernization.

Rawane's Song 2006, an autobiographical video by Mounira Al Solh, is a witty take on her struggle to make work about the Lebanese wars in the wake of the previous generation of Beirut artists. Ironically it ends up addressing exactly the issues she claims to be avoiding.

Slavs and Tatars' practice examines a region they describe as 'east of the former Berlin Wall and west of the Great Wall of China'. Their text-based works and installations draw on a variety of sources and play with double-meanings, mistranslation, language barriers and notions of the dichotomy between east and west."

Although the sign displays a different meaning to the exhibit, I interpret it totally different. I interpret this as a message to the public to literally not save the world. People know that Christianity uses the term "save" meaning to save souls.

The exhibit reflected:
- A child on a video when you first enter saying, "I decided not to save the world",
- Pictures on the wall of a hand with fingers moving over a wall
- A video playing on the wall of a documentary about a woman who wanted to save a country and just gave up
- A video on the floor of a child using scissors to cut through water

All of the above begs the onlooker to question fighting for a cause. It leaves the impression that Christians are fighting a losing war for souls. It implies to the world to just give up and not to try.

This exhibit is anti-Christian rhetoric to discourage people from trying to save souls. The videos show a child doing the actions which is a mockery of the Christian faith in that the Bible says to come to Jesus as child-like faith. The palm tree with lights in it is a reflection of the burned out bulbs within it; meaning the Christians should give up trying to be a light unto the world.

The Energy and Process Exhibit is strange to me. The picture of the triangle with many shapes on the corners I interpret as the triangle is lopsided with many shapes and forms on each. The top picture shows a human figure in the midst of the triangle shapes. To me, this relays the message of a person hid within the message of society, which could relate to urban life. The second picture is a reflection of society back in the 1960s with cartoons. The third picture is a statue with a hammerhead and a cross over it. The statue looks like he is marching forward to battle. This statue is an imitation of a Christian warmonger - of a negative light. My interpretation however does not match how the museum describes this artwork completed in 1917. The museum says, "..depicts a figure in motion, aerodynamically deformed by speed."

States of Flux Exhibit is designed for artist to show the world the complex reality of modern life and the machine age of art. The meaning is to relay the message of the visual revolution. The sign outside the exhibit says, "The wing also features work by contemporary artists who continue to generate new ways of depicting and understanding urban life."

CHILDHOOD MUSEUM

The Stuff of Nightmares Exhibit is hard to understand. The displays were creepy and especially creepy considering children would be looking at this stuff. One display had a black crow holding a dead baby in a cloth. This is like the stork delivering a dead baby. I consider the movie *The Birds*. I also think of the movie *Rosemary's Baby*. Another display is like death coming to the mother and is like evil being placed upon the baby. Very strange.

It is amazing that nearly six months later at the opening ceremonies of the London Olympics, they did a section like this where children were lying in bed having nightmares and being chased around like demons. So, not only are they displaying this mindset in museums, but now showing it at the Olympics.

We learned in class that if you continually tell a story or idea it will stick. In other words, repetition is key in changing habits and engagement.

NATIONAL MARITIME MUSEUM

High Arctic Exhibit: Future Visions of a Receding World is an attempt to bring validity to the global warming agenda of the new world order. The exhibit is described as "a genuinely immersive, responsive environment," The sign reads, "High Arctic is a UVA Creative Director Matt Clark's response to his experience of the Arctic as part of Cape Farewell's 2010 expedition. Set in AD2100, in a future where the Arctic environment has changed forever, High Arctic acts as a monument to a lost world. Sound, light and sculptural forms create an immersive landscape for visitors to explore, conveying the scale, beauty and fragility of today's Arctic and encouraging us to question our relationship with the world around us."

This exhibit is a hidden message to society of global warming. I do not believe they enacted the exhibit properly in that it is too confusing to the people. I asked the worker inside and he agreed saying it is too confusing for people. I understand the concept of the glaciers from beginning to end with having the glacier names on each block so that the person can keep up with it from beginning to end, but the light show is confusing.

HAMPTON COURT CASTLE

Throughout the castle of King Henry VIII, I notice Anne Bolyn did not get the recognition she deserves. I kept noticing throughout the tour of the castle the missing information about Anne and I asked one of the workers about it and he said they chose to give Katherine more glory than Anne. Anne caused King Henry to break away from the Catholic Church and become protestant. Could this be a tactic to diminish the accomplishments of Queen Elizabeth? In our textbook, this type of omission is reflected as an illusion to the truth.

A GLOBAL TOWER OF BABEL

I participated in CCSA Study Abroad program in the winter of 2011/2012. While in London, I had the honor of receiving training from the top global communication, advertising, and public relations firms in the world. The supremacy I sensed was remarkable. Through the vast connections with their campaigns, they can literally change the world and cultures.

The commonality between the three firms is the vast representatives of many different cultures and backgrounds together in one building representing the numerous target audiences. These firms also merged all technologies in one building such as video, audio, social media, printing, editing, etc. In other words, they have the top minds in unity for a purpose. In the Christian world, we say, "In one mind and one accord."

These firms utilize everything in the marketing mix as their strategies. They cover every aspect of a campaign to affect the communications industry. These organizations have the capacity to maximize their marketing potential. This is a powerful force. Each of those firms is a Tower of Babel within its own communications right.

The Internet has opened the door to today's Biblical Tower of Babel increasing the flow of information on Earth. "It is estimated Internet users would double by 2015 to a global total of some four billion users, or nearly 60 percent of Earth's population." (UNCP.edu 2012).

Mooji (2010) reports, "The Internet by its very nature is a global communications channel, with the potential to reach consumers anywhere in the world". Imagine a world where the Internet no longer exists only on a machine but totally in people, animals, and highways. RFID technology for the future is here.

With RFID technology, it provides avenues to gather data from all over the world. It is a tool to unite humankind through computers, chips, tags, and other devices of RFID. This is a Biblical Tower of Babel as well because the masterminds are trying to interconnect all of society to control every aspect of it. Hitler could not have done it without the technology and IBM.

SELLING THE MARK OF THE BEAST

WHAT IS THE CHIP/RFID TAG?

The human implantation device is known as an RFID tag. It is more popularly known as the chip. This device is quickly implanted under the skin of humans. Animals have been implanted for more than a decade now.

RFID is produced by a company called Applied Digital Solutions and funded by IBM. (Business Editors, 2003). The radio frequency identification devices come in many forms. They are chips that can be imbedded into humans, animals, clothing, food, products, packaging, computers, and almost anything you can imagine. The definition in the London Transport Museum: (IT Museum, 2012)

In America, VeriChip is the main corporation that produced the chip. In 2009, the company changed its name to PositiveID Corporation. "About the size of a grain of rice, each VeriChip product contains a unique verification number that is captured by briefly passing a proprietary scanner over the VeriChip. A small amount of radio frequency energy passes from the scanner energizing the dormant VeriChip emits a radio frequency signal transmitting the verification number.

In October 2002, the US Food and Drug Administration (FDA) ruled that VeriChip is not a regulated device with regard to its security, financial, personal identification/ safety applications but that VeriChip's healthcare information applications are regulated by the FDA. VeriChip Corporation is a wholly owned subsidiary of Applied Digital Solutions (Nasdaq: ADSX)." (Business Editors, 2003).

VeriChip faced challenges from watchdog groups and privacy activists for years. The mountains of bad publicity and the misleading of information to the media about its products led the organization into a frenzy to redefine itself.

In a marketing ploy, the company changed its name to a more positive one, PositiveID. PositiveID is located in Delray Beach, Florida. (PositiveID, 2012).

One goal of the implantation of the RFID chip is to implant every citizen. As this article explains, "The alliance brings PositiveID one step closer to its dream of having as many Americans as possible volunteer to have a microchip surgically implanted under their skin that will link to an online database containing their medical records". (Edwards, 2010). This company is presenting it in this article as desiring to only include medical records, however, the real goal is to control every area of your life through this chip – finances, your health system inside your body, and your location at all times, and access to all your data.

RFID comes in many forms such as nano-sized, to sizes like grains of rice, to small computer chips, etc. RFID technology is credited to improving supply-chain management as well. An example of this is with Walmart. Let's say Walmart orders shirts from a manufacturer. The clothing is embedded with RFID tags. Through readers, Walmart can track that shirt from production to the life cycle. They can tell everywhere that shirt travels by tracking it. This product is how stores are able to efficiently track their merchandise. It is also scary for the consumer because we do not know how they turn it off when we purchase it or if they continue to track what happens with that product once you purchase it.

On my website, www.norfidchip.com, I provide more information about RFID technology and newer updated information. Please check it out and research it further.

CHALLENGES OF SELLING TO CHRISTIANS

The most challenging market segment to sell this product is Christians. "A market segment is a set of businesses or group of individual consumers with distinct characteristics." (Baack, 2010). Christians will not allow anything to be inserted under their skin that will participate in the world's system of transactions, tracking services, or health records. They will consider this technology the Mark of the Beast as told in the book of Revelation. (The End Times News, 2012).

Some critics may say the Bible refers to worshiping the beast and it does not relate to the mark, however, if a person takes a computer chip under their skin to participate in buying and selling through the world's system, then that is the mark of the beast.

This form of mark is considered worshiping the beast and his system on Earth. The Bible foretold the prophecy years ago and most Christians would strictly adhere to its instructions.

In order to sell a product successfully, a company must engage the target audience to act upon their agenda through the advertisement or media plan. It is known that in order to engage your target audience you must bring in trust. How do we present an idea to a target audience that is dead-set against your product or idea? The company must collaborate with key leaders in that demographic and enlist their help. The Christians that follow tradition and man instead of the Word of God may be more susceptible to taking the mark versus Christians who believe the Bible as the inerrant truth.

Society and culture are great influencers when it comes to selling products. Later in this book, I will explain why a product such as a computer chip under the skin may sell better in Europe versus selling it in the United States. There are many different variables involved in these scenarios.

As I visited the London Transport Museum's *Sense in the City* exhibit and discovered a near future where all society has chips. This was shocking to me considering my history with Christianity. In addition, it was not just this exhibit; it was in almost every museum. Each place had different elements displaying the Antichrist spirit and one-world innuendos. I must warn people.

MARKETING OF THE AGES: WHAT BROUGHT US TO THIS POINT?

Our school textbook explains, "Globalization in the broadest sense is best defined as 'the crystallization of the entire world in a single place" (Mooji, 2010, Pg. 6). How does a society agree to be in one place? How can we shape events to turn all civilization to one world peaceful union? The answer is through a group called the Illuminati, as some conspiracy theorists suggest. The Illuminati is a secret society born in the1776 and temporarily dismantled in the late 1790s in Bavaria. (The Masons, 2009). Some conspiracy theorists believe this group shaped the course of events even to our current day. Considering my thoughts on the Tower of Babel and intellectual minds converging, this theory only makes sense. It has to be a group of world leaders coming together to agree on certain outcomes.

Consider the role IBM plays in our history. IBM is connected to Hitler's agenda in World War II in that IBM helped Hitler kill the Jews. IBM provided his regime with the machines, census materials, and the gas to kill the Jews. (ACSA, 2003). How else could Hitler kill millions of Jews without being organized by machines? It was a very organized slaughter of humanity. With IBM assisting with that genocide and them financially backing the new technology of RFID and global implantation, will history not repeat itself? I say it will. IBM has a commercial about RFID technology in which a man is appearing to steal merchandise and walk out the door without security stopping him. This video is to show the capabilities of RFID technology. (YouTube, 2006).

In order to shape society to accept the technology of RFID, some global force or group must retrain society's views toward accepting this technology. If you review history and consider how events happened, it makes it clear how we got to this point. The global forces were behind WWII. Even America used propaganda to persuade the citizens to support the war.

When Hitler reigned, he was loved in the beginning. He did not start out instructing to kill Jews. His regime set his building on fire and told the citizens it was communist. He brainwashed his people to accept this as a way to protect their society. He accomplished his agenda through fear and loyalty. As we learned in our textbook, emotions play a huge part in marketing a product. To market Hitler's agenda he used propaganda to persuade his people. The same is happening today with Obama's agenda. Several authors have written books about the media's love affair with Obama and the media purposefully ignoring his evil agenda.

What happened in our society since WWII? We entered the Cold War where people lived in fear and built bomb shelters, etc. "The Cold War kept the world on edge for over 50 years. People built bomb shelters in their back yards and schoolchildren practiced a-bomb drills. Nuclear war seemed inevitable. Under that shadow of a potential holocaust, the NATO and Warsaw Pact (or Eastern Bloc) nations twisted and turned to advance their goals while avoiding the spark that might instigate a war of surpassing destruction." (Academic American, No Date). According to this article, the government used this fear to pass laws infringing on Americans.

Our society changed in the area of religion around this time also. We began taking God out of our schools slowly to where now Christians are being persecuted for having Bibles on their desks. (Accountability in the Media, 2009). In other words, government took over the education sector, which slowly worked towards changing the mindsets of future generations. By changing textbooks to a secular worldview, it attempts to instill in its readers this humanistic worldview. Some of the textbooks I have had in college spoke a lot about events of the past being Christian's fault and heavily played on white guilt. White guilt meaning the white man is painted in a negative light, or been placed as the guilty ones. The textbooks our children are subjected to add to the reshaping of the minds to the generations.

Marketing professionals target demographics according to generations. For instance, there is Generation X, Generation Y, the Baby Boomers, etc. We target those separate generations because the worldview of those decades changed. "Segmentation based on generations notes that as people experience significant external events during their late adolescence or early adulthood, these events impact their social values, attitudes, and preferences." (Baack, 2010).

The worldview presented to those populations is impartations such as the media exposure of the age, the technology, the education, the world events, and the religious patterns of society. Understanding how different generations think greatly enhances the marketing potential. So, if a group can control the current events globally, the media, the education and text we are reading, the technology and laws to affect religions, then how would that affect society? It will push a certain agenda in the intended direction for the future plan. This is the plan of the Illuminati.

For instance, former president John F. Kennedy presented a speech in 1963, one week before he was assassinated, in which he warned the American public about the New World Order. In his speech he said, "The very word "secrecy" is repugnant in a free and open society; and we are as a people inherently and historically opposed to secret societies, to secret oaths and to secret proceedings." (YouTube, 2007).

He also describes in his speech how this group's goal is infiltration versus subversion. Considering his speech, it makes the point clear that the New World Order agenda is to infiltrate our society. How? It is through education, the media, and world events to drive fear to the people.

He was assassinated a week after this speech.

Another world event that shaped our society is the Vietnam War. Some people feel we did not have a right to be over there to begin with. Because of our involvement in this war, it brought more fear to the nations. Following that war was the Iraq and Kuwait War. This was the first step as labeling terrorism. Terrorism is a made up term to describe an organization or group that opposes governments. Even Janet Napolitano, Secretary of Homeland Defense, after she first was in office labeled Christians as "home-grown terrorists." She did not outright say Christians, but she described a person who did not support abortions or illegals. The main religion against those practices is Christianity. Napolitano especially targeted war veterans. (Hudson, 2009).

Another questionable world event is 9/11. The government and media wants society to believe that airplanes were hijacked by Muslim terrorists and the Twin Towers fell due to the crash.

Some "truthers" say the towers were taken down by a demolition team in addition to the planes. Strong evidence exists to dispute the government's perspective of the event. However, whether it is a real event or a forged event by the government to set the stage for the New World Order, it is evident that American rights have been stripped to the bone since that event. The government passed the Patriot Act, which allowed the government to pry into our personal lives. Our country has spiraled out of control since that event. Our civil liberties are under attack due to fear in the people.

Back to London: I took this picture in London. In the picture above, please notice the camera in front of the store and a camera on the side of the store. Also, on the front of the icebox is a yellow sign saying, "Watch" with a big eye picture. This is a message to the community they are being watched by the store and to not steal from this store. In addition to the cameras is an ADT box on the side of the building, which alerts the customers this store has security. The people in London are so comfortable with cameras.

This is in the Tube in London. Please notice the two cameras at the top of the picture and the speakers on the ceiling. This man singing at the bottom of the elevator is the transportation industry sending a message to the people that they celebrate culture. This is to make their experience in the tube less disturbing with all of the cameras and hidden microphones all over the place.

It is creepy in the underground because there are cameras every five feet and hidden microphones all over the ceilings to monitor people's conversations. To alleviate some of the citizen's paranoia, they have random performers to sing. It is all an allusion.

I also believe that the television show *Big Brother* and reality shows are designed to desensitize us to the invasion of the government and prying eyes. If we pay attention to the latest movies about this type of thing like *Hunger Games* and *The Cabin in the Woods*.

Hunger Games is a reality-based show where people in villages must sacrifice one of their children to the television show once a year to fight to the death for food. Once a candidate is chosen, then the world watches as that candidate struggles to survive the harsh circumstances. It shows them in a dome where the elements are controlled by the powers-that-be.

The Cabin in the Woods is based upon these characters going to a cabin in the woods for vacation. They have no idea they are in a reality show. It shows zombies coming after them and very weird circumstances. Once the few make it back to society, they realize they are within a reality show and then demons are released as onlookers watch the horror.

I could go on and on about the various television shows and the mind control within them. One I do want to mention is *The Purge*. This movie is about allowing evil to reign for a certain amount of time once a year. They want to give the impression to the world that we should let the beast out once in a while. It is just plain evil.

Anyways, please notice how Hollywood has been engrossed in the gay movement agenda. Almost every television show has gay or homosexual characters in it. One of my favorite shows, *Nashville*, has a gay country music artist. My point to all of this is that the powers-that-be want you to accept this lifestyle as normal and OK (not like how the Bible declares it). They are brainwashing society to believe their doctrine.

As the Bible says, what comes in will come out. Be careful what comes in your eye gate and ear gate. We must protect our hearts.

SELLING THE MARK OF THE BEAST

AGENDA SETTING THEORY

In the communications industry, we have many different theories about how communication is processed in our cultures. In my opinion, the media is structured according to the Agenda Setting Theory where the information released to the public is set by a certain group of people. I am referring to the mainstream media. All of their news stories are on the same subjects the majority of the time.

An example of media operating with clear agendas is in London. Their children's television shows are about kings, queens, knights and everything to do with the monarchy. These shows are both cartoons and regular shows. The media in London paints the monarchy as a normal, peaceful lifestyle. In America, our cartoons and children's shows are nothing like that. Our shows are individualistic and sometimes rebellious towards authority.

As I am reading the newspapers from Europe, I begin to notice a pattern. The message the media is relaying to the readers is an obvious support for the U.S. Presidential Candidate Mitt Romney. In the communications industry, we call this the Agenda Setting Theory. This theory suggests the media is trying to sway public opinion. These papers are from various companies. Europe being a "big brother" country, this obvious influx of support for Romney tells me that big brother wants him to win. In other words, the "elite" want Romney to win the Republican nomination. Christians do not like Romney and it would hurt the Christian fight if Romney won. In addition, Romney is another form of Obama such as his support of Obama's new bill that would not give Americans due process if they were arrested as a terrorist. This is a dangerous bill because what if the government finds Christians as terrorists. Janet Napolitano adds Christians in her "homegrown terrorists" description.

Another example of media difference between the UK and US is an exhibit in London at the Imperial War Museum. This exhibit displays British service members who served in Afghanistan. The whole exhibit painted their experience in a positive light. In America, we hear a different story. We mostly hear about the negative impact of the war.

In the UK, they do not have as many reality television shows we have in the United States. In the United States, the media keeps distracted with senseless media such as reality TV. American Idol is a great example with millions of viewers. While we are engrossed in our senseless television shows, President Obama is signing our rights away with such bills as the NDAA (National Defense Authorization Act).

Within this bill it allows our government to hold American Citizens without the possibility of a fair trial, which our constitution safeguards. (Morrill, 2011) Instead of the media bringing this story to the forefront and its full potential, they focus on Obama fighting for the rights of insurance companies to pay for contraception. This subject is trivial compared to the constitution invasion from our president.

The media also does not bring it to the forefront about the truth and the plan of human implantation of the chips. For instance, when Sarah Palin ran on the McCain ticket for vice president in 2008, the media tore her to shreds because she is a Christian and conservative. The media wore her out and even attacked her children's character. Why do they not do the same to Obama? Is there a bigger agenda? I believe it is.

Some conspiracy theorists believe the United States government is already preparing concentration camps for the future. In addition, the fact that Obama is preparing the army to handle U.S. civilians in the case of martial law is enough to alarm U.S. citizens. (The National Inflation Association, 2011). According to this article, the mainstream media is ignoring this.

In the transportation industry in London, they began a new payment system called the Oyster card. This card scans over a sensor and it makes the transaction faster when entering or exiting the tube station. The yellow circle object on top of the ticket box is the Oyster card sensor.

The patron scans their card quickly when they walk through. The message this is sending the patrons is how easy and convenient it is to not deal with paper tickets anymore and how fast it is to just scan quickly. This is in preparation for RFID chip in human hands. In the future people can just walk through the scanner and only be required to scan their hand. This is described in our text as one of the seven forms of advertising. This form is association transfer in Lesson 2.1.

Another proof that the plans are to turn the world against Christians is when I interviewed two London Transport employees about the RFID. I asked them if they heard of it and they replied "No." I explained how the London Oyster Card has an RFID chip inside it and they said it makes sense. They also informed me of a startling fact that the media does not cover.

Those two employees informed me that Muslim women kill themselves and their children at an alarming rate in The Tube (the underground transportation train). They said the women just grab their children and jump in front of the trains when they are moving at a fast speed. I inquired as to the media's coverage of this startling fact and they replied they do not report on it. Why does the media purposefully hide this fact from its citizens but is quick to paint Christians negatively?

Agenda Setting can also be seen in the textbooks, as I previously mentioned. Consider who the one segment the marketers of RFID will not be able to penetrate with their plan. Knowing what the scripture says and how the Christians will not accept that technology, they must implement a plan to turn the rest of society against Christians. By turning society against this segment, it opens the door for persecution against Christians and the removal of that hindrance. To the Christian, if they take this technology (representing the mark of the beast), it dooms their soul to Hell. They will not participate in this agenda.

How do they turn society against a people who are majority peaceful people?

They start on them when they are children.

Teach them creation does not exist.

Teach them Christianity is the reason all of the Indians died in early America history.

Teach them how they treated the slaves in times past. Turn them against that religion through textbooks and public school.

Setup places in museums to show children how bad Christianity is such as the Hitler display at the Imperial War Museum in London.

As you entered the museum, a movie is playing and says, "Christians were taught in their religion to hate Jews because they killed Jesus." This documentary is to explain to the public why Hitler killed the millions of Jews. (YouTube, 2012).

In addition, the museum displays a measuring rod where Hitler's minions would measure heads to test if they were authentically of white descent. This paints a negative picture of white people to onlookers.

Other examples include visiting the Tate Modern Museum in London. This museum displayed an exhibit called *I Decided Not to Save the World*. You will experience a video playing when you enter the exhibit with a child repeating those fateful words. On the wall are several pictures of fingers skipping over a wall. This signifies not trying to fight the system, but merely crossing over it. (YouTube, 2012). It is the subtle ambiances over time that shapes a child's mind.

All forms of media shape a generation. To change a worldview it will take all forms of marketing tactics. As I said previously about the marketing mix, it takes all forms to change a mind like visual, audio, experiences, etc. The Bible says, "Raise a child in the way he should go and he will not depart from it." (Proverbs 22:6).

Through textbooks infiltrating the influential young minds of liberal doctrine and ideology, the younger generation is ready to accept a questionable president, in-spite of his detrimental faults such as terrorist connections, his questionable birth certificate issue, his heritage in Indonesia in Islam School, etc. The media twisted the communication to the public by accusing every negative statement against the president being racist. The youth of the nation supported him and did not consider his history like the older generations. The media created this president. This is an example of Agenda Setting Theory's success.

MARKETING THE RFID: EU VS. US

With the ultimate plan being to chip or tag all of society like cattle; each culture is required to approach their segments in their respective protocols. Marketing this product to Europe is different than marketing it to civilians in the United States. One reason it will vary is due to the religious culture.

The culture in Europe is not as conservative in Christianity as America. Europe is more consumerism and materialistic than Americans. This opinion is based upon my three-week experience in Europe and studying their media and culture. Based upon my visit to the Olympic area in London, I knew they would incorporate the latest consumerism mentality utilizing current technology into the event. At the Olympics during both the opening and closing show, they practically worshipped Satan with all the occultism in the symbolism. It was a very satanic show.

The European Union is majority Catholic and the Church of England. The actual percentage of protestant faith is small compared to other religions according to the European Union website. (Eupedia, 2012). Due to this fact, the European Union is on a faster pace with marketing this human implantation device than the United States. With their society more worldly than the U.S., the job of the marketers is not as hard. Their main obstacle is the privacy issue.

The European Commission is a group formed by the governments to organize the unions. The EC is currently promoting RFID human implantation through videos, fun events with the public and instructional seminars across the region. This committee has implemented several marketing strategies to promote this change of technology with society. The EU already trained their society to accept Big Brother watching them at all times with video cameras everywhere and a very worldview towards life. For instance, their worldly pleasures of shopping are so obsessive that their advertising speaks to the level of worship to material things.

Our study abroad group visited an advertising firm, which presented advertising examples they have utilized in Europe. On one advertisement is two women fighting over a sale at this high-end retail store and one of the women has a demon protruding out of her stomach with a sword in her hand. She is in a karate-style formation ready to fight the other woman over the products in the store.

This type of advertising is not practiced in the United States because Americans are too conservative. I can imagine the multitudes accepting the chip if the EU offered the chip just to save the citizens from their credit card being stolen.

The European Union is advertising through video to encourage citizens to participate in this new RFID system. One video portrays a country much safer and more convenience brought to their society. The European Commission has a warmly colored website to answer any questions.

To address the marketing strategy of the EC, they created another tactic called the Internet of Things. (Europa, 2011). The Internet of Things is a term used to describe a society where everything has internet and is interconnected. Humans are connected to machines, machines are adapted into the human world versus the humans adapting to it. Machines are becoming smarter and IBM is behind all of this technology. Even IBM has a commercial titled the Internet of Things. (YouTube, 2010). These videos are cute little cartoon characters explaining the meaning of The Internet of Things.

In contrast, the United States has given much resistance to the new technology. Activist and watchdog groups have fought this change for over a decade. The media in America overshadows this subject with an influx of entertainment such as movies, games, and sports. The media chooses to focus on superficial news such as Kim Kardashian and other trivial gossip-trains.

Europe does not have the luxuries we have with entertainment. Our Internet technology is better, we have more television shows, and more sports to keep us entertained while the government secretly plans this RFID overhaul.

In Obama's Healthcare Reform, he inserted legislation to enforce the medical industry to adapt their industry to conform to the RFID standards. Beginning on page 1013, he instructs the medical industry they have 36 months to prepare their hospitals and offices with RFID scanners and materials to plan for the implementation of the human implantation of humans. This enforcement of human implantable chips will begin in March of 2013. (U.S. House, 2010). America is not even aware of this plan. Some are, but if they talk about it, they are considered conspiracy theorist and ignored. This plan was stopped by watchdog groups before implementation in 2013, but is apparently scheduled for 2017. Either way, this is a classic example of how the watchdog groups stop legislation from steam rolling through our society. I encourage you to research it more as far as the implementation date.

This is the difference between the European Union and the United States. We pass bills without even reading them because of the dark agenda behind them. How will they get Americans to go along with it? There may be a disastrous event that will cause them to want to do it out of fear, or an economic collapse.

Another reason may be an outbreak of disease. America is taking the soft road to selling this product because our text explains, "Masculinity/femininity reflects the division between countries in which hype and the hard sell prevail versus countries where a soft-sell, more modest approach is successful." (Mooji, 2010). Our culture is more feminine in that men work part-time to help the women and do without the masculinity role such as Europe in their relationships.

Most Christians will not buy into the idea of the RFID human implantable Chip because they know the Bible foretold these events. They also realize this strategy is part of the bigger picture of the New World Order or one-world government. The Bible speaks about the one-world government as ushering in the Antichrist and the false prophet of Satan.

The marketers and designers of this plan know they will have tremendous challenges marketing this to the Christian market. Their plan is to turn the world against this religion so that when the time comes to implement this globally, great persecution will come on the Christians because they will not participate in this global agenda. Their first order of business must be to shape the minds of the citizens to accept their plan and anyone who does not participate in that plan will be eliminated.

The Bible speaks of elimination for not taking the mark. "I saw thrones on which were seated those who had been given authority to judge. And I saw the souls of those who had been beheaded because of their testimony for Jesus and because of the word of God. They had not worshiped the beast or his image and had not received his mark on their foreheads or their hands. They came to life and reigned with Christ a thousand years." (Revelation 20:4).

SPIRITUAL COST OF THE MARK

As a minister of the gospel, I must explain the cost of accepting the mark of the beast and the worldly system. Taking the mark is more than just spiritual death; it is the ultimate separation from God. Our bodies are the temple of the Holy Ghost. We have been bought with a price. I will try to explain...

In the beginning, we were created by God in the Garden of Eden. He created us from the dirt and He blew into us and created our spirits. God walked with Adam and Eve in the garden and told them not to eat of the Tree of Knowledge of Good and Evil. He told them to eat from the Tree of Life. When Eve and Adam ate from the wrong tree, their spirit man inside died. They were dead men walking. The same thing will happen to us now if we take the mark. We may still be living, but our souls will be dead.

When Jesus came to Earth, He paid for our redemption by dying on the cross and becoming the sacrificial lamb for our sins. He bought us with the highest price, His life. Through this sacrifice, his blood, He opened up the way for us to have living spirits again. By Him being resurrected, it opened the way for the Holy Spirit to come and live on the inside of us. We are now the temple of the Living God. Our temples are not made with stone, but with flesh.

In addition, we are the Bride of Christ. When we receive Jesus' sacrifice and accept his salvation, then He has purchased us with His blood. We are delivered out of this world's plan and enter into His Heavenly plan. We are a world within this world.

So, if we allow the world to literally buy back the rights that Satan stole from Adam by allowing them to insert a tag into our flesh and break blood with Satan, then we literally reverse what Jesus did.

Accepting the mark of the beast is more than just accepting a chip underneath our skin, it is accepting the worldly system's way of living. We are selling our soul to Satan when we accept the world to implant into our temples the computer chip that will relay this temple's activity. See, when we are full of the Holy Ghost and power, we allow the Holy Ghost to have full control of this temple. God's Heavenly laws and it trumps the worldly system.

If we take the chip, then we are literally committing adultery against our husband, Jesus, and committing the ultimate act of abomination. We are stomping on Jesus' head and saying, "We do not accept your sacrifice anymore because it will cost ME too much. I'd rather have it made on Earth and not suffer temporarily." We are literally making that choice with this decision.

All of our relationship with God is based upon decisions. We decide to get saved. We decide to turn from the devil. We decide to not follow the appetites of the flesh and follow God no matter the cost. Therefore, this decision may be the last one you make on this Earth. We must be willing to die for His name and be His true bride. This is the most beautiful love story ever written.

He died for us and we are WILLING to die for Him *if our decision so requires*. **We will not accept Satan's mark on or within our temples at any cost.**

To be saved today, say this prayer with me:

> *Father God, I accept Jesus Christ's sacrifice for my sins. I believe He died on the cross for me and please forgive me for all my sins. I believe you rose from the dead on the third day. Holy Spirit you are welcome in my temple and use me for your glory. In Jesus' name, Amen!*

REFERENCES

Academic American. (No Date). *America and the Cold War*. Retrieved February 18, 2012, from: http://www.academicamerican.com/postww2/coldwar.html

Accountability in the Media. (2009, March 26). *"Bible on the Desk" Teacher Was Singled Out, Witness Said*. Retrieved February 18, 2012, from: http://www.accountabilityinthemedia.com/2009/03/bible-on-desk-teacher-was-singled-out.html

ACSA. (2003, July 13). IBM Caused WWII. Retrieved February 18, 2012, from: http://www.acsa.net/ibm_and_hitler.htm

Baack, C. (2010). *Integrated Advertising, Promotion, and Marketing Communication*. New Jersey: Pearson Education.

Business Editors. (2003, June 30). *Applied Digital Solutions Makes $30 Million Payment to IBM Credit, LLC, Satisfying All Outstanding Debt Obligations to IBM*. Retrieved February 17, 2012, from: http://www.thefreelibrary.com/Applied+Digital+Solutions+Makes+%2430+Million+Payment+to+IBM+Credit%2c..-a0104535532

Curtis, Dr. Anthony, (2012) Social Media History. Retrieved from: http://www2.uncp.edu/home/acurtis/NewMedia/SocialMedia/SocialMediaHistory.html

Edwards, J. (2009, November 11). *VeriChip Buys Steel Vault, Creating Micro-Implant Health Record/Credit Score Empire*. Retrieved February 18, 2012, from: http://www.cbsnews.com/news/verichip-buys-steel-vault-creating-micro-implant-health-record-credit-score-empire/

Edwards, J. (2010, November 09). *Positive ID Deal Advances Use of Microchip Implants in Florida Health System*. Retrieved December 27, 2014, from: http://www.cbsnews.com/news/positiveid-deal-advances-use-of-microchip-implants-in-florida-health-system/

Eupedia. (2012). Maps of Europe. Retrieved January 18, 2012, from: http://www.eupedia.com/europe/maps_of_europe.shtml#religions

Europa. (2011, March 28). European Research Cluster on the Internet of Things. Retrieved February 18, 2012, from: http://cordis.europa.eu/fp7/ict/enet/rfid-iot_en.html

Fairchild, M. (No Date). About.com: Christianity. Retrieved February 18, 2012, from: http://abt.cm/19Fzcrz

Hudson, A. a. (2009, April 14). *Federal Agency Warns of Radicals on Right*. Retrieved February 18, 2012, from: http://www.washingtontimes.com/news/2009/apr/14/federal-agency-warns-of-radicals-on-right/

LT Museum. (2012). *Exhibition: Sense and the City*. Retrieved February 18, 2012, from London Transport Museum: http://www.ltmuseum.co.uk/whats-on/exhibitions/171-exhibition-sense-and-the-city

Mooji, M. D. (2010). *Global Marketing and Advertising.* Thousand Oaks, California: Sage.

Morrill, J. (2011, December 31). *Obama Signs NDAA Law, Dismantling Bill of Rights*. Retrieved February 18, 2012, from: http://www.examiner.com/independent-in-salt-lake-city/obama-signs-ndaa-into-law-dismantles-bill-of-rights?CID=obinsite

Positive I.D. (2012). *Contact Us*. Retrieved February 18, 2012, from: http://www.positiveidcorp.com/contact.html

The End Times News. (2012, February 09). *The Technology For The Mark Of The Beast Is Here Now - Smart Skin*. Retrieved February 18, 2012, from: http://www.tldm.org/news4/markofthebeast.htm

The Masons. (2009, 29 August). The Illuminati. Retrieved February 18, 2012, from: http://www.masonicinfo.com/illuminati.htm

PR Newswire. (2011, September 07). *Obama Preparing for Martial Law During Hyperinflation*. Retrieved February 18, 2012, from: http://www.prnewswire.com/news-releases/obama-preparing-for-martial-law-during- hyperinflation-says-nia-129425123.html

U.S. House. (2010, March 17). H.R. 4872. Retrieved February 18, 2012, from: http://housedocs.house.gov/rules/hr4872/111_hr4872_reported.pdf

YouTube. (2006, June 02). *IBM RFID Commercial: The Future Supermarket*. Retrieved February 16, 2012, from: http://www.youtube.com/watch?v=eob532iEpqk

YouTube. (2007, July 30). *President John F Kennedy Secret Society Speech version 2*. Retrieved February 18, 2012, from: http://youtu.be/xhZk8ronces

YouTube. (2010, November 30). *IBM - Track Everything - The Internet of Things*. Retrieved September 18, 2012, from: http://youtu.be/RkJjJfD59Pk

YouTube. (2012, January 20). *Christians Are Blamed for the Holocaust in Imperial War Museum*. Retrieved January 20, 2012, from: http://youtu.be/1g3aexrB4a4?list=UUje_VZDbsIaErsvDRwV8fQQ

YouTube. (2012, January 20). *I Decided Not To Save The World*. Retrieved February 18, 2012, from: http://youtu.be/A3Q9enf9Yq8

The pictures were taken by June in London. June Dawn Knight has all rights to the pictures.

www.gotreehouse.org (Publisher)
www.norfidchip.com (Website in addition to book)
www.junedawn.com (More about author)

LONDON CREDITS

London Transport Museum
http://www.ltmuseum.co.uk/
Covent Garden Piazza
London
WC2E 7BB

National Maritime Museum
http://www.nmm.ac.uk/
Romney Road
Greenwich, SE10 9NF
+44 (0)20 8858 4422

Hampton Court (Henry VIII's Castle)
http://www.hrp.org.uk/HamptonCourtPalace/
London Borough of Richmond upon Thames, Greater London

Children's Museum
http://www.childrensmuseum.org.uk/
18 Broadwick St, London W1F 8HS

London Science Museum
http://www.sciencemuseum.org.uk/
Exhibition Road
South Kensington
SW7 2DD

The Imperial War Museum
http://www.iwm.org.uk/
IWM Duxford
Cambridgeshire CB22 4QR

Tate Modern
http://www.tate.org.uk/modern/
Bankside
London SE1 9TG

Made in the USA
Charleston, SC
08 March 2015